ZOOM IN ON BUTTERFLIES

Melissa Stewart

ZOOM In on Insects!

E Enslow Elementary

CONTENTS

WORDS TO KNOW

chrysalis (KRIS uh liss)—The hard outer skin of a butterfly pupa.

larva (LAHR vuh)—The second part in the life cycle of some insects. A butterfly larva is called a caterpillar. A larva changes into a pupa.

nectar (NEK tuhr)—A sugary liquid that many flowers make. Butterflies and some other insects drink it.

pupa (PYOO puh)—The third part in the life cycle of some insects. A pupa changes into an adult.

BUTTERFLY HOMES

ZOOM BUBBLE

Butterflies live in many parts of the world. But they can't live in dry, hot deserts.

In places with cold winters, some butterflies fly to warmer areas. Others rest in safe spots all winter long.

PARTS OF A BUTTERFLY

wing

antennae

head

eye

thorax

leg

abdomen

BUTTERFLY BODY

ZOOM BUBBLE

A butterfly is an insect. An insect has six legs. Its body has three main parts. An insect's head is in the front. The thorax is in the middle. The abdomen is the part at the back.

BUTTERFLY EYES

ZOOM BUBBLE

A butterfly has two huge eyes. They stick out of its head. The eyes can see right and left, up and down—all at the same time. What a great trick!

BUTTERFLY ANTENNAE

ZOOM BUBBLE

A butterfly has two long antennae on the top of its head. They can move up and down or side to side. They smell and feel the world.

BUTTERFLY TONGUES

ZOOM BUBBLE

Most butterflies get all their food from flowers. They sip sweet nectar with a long, thin tongue. It works like a drinking straw. Some butterflies suck juices from rotting fruit. Others drink sap from a tree.

BUTTERFLY WINGS

ZOOM BUBBLE

A butterfly has two sets of wings. It uses the wings to fly from place to place.

Why do butterflies need to fly? To find lots of food and to lay their eggs in good spots.

The butterfly in the top photo
blends into the tree.
The blue butterfly is bright and stands out!

BUTTERFLY SCALES

ZOOM BUBBLE

A butterfly has a thin, smooth coat of scales on its wings. They look like the shingles on a roof. The scales give the wings their colors. Some wings are bright and beautiful. Others blend in with leaves or tree bark.

BUTTERFLY LEGS

ZOOM BUBBLE

A butterfly has six legs. They are attached to the middle of its body.

A butterfly can rest on its legs. But it can't walk very well. Hairs on its feet can taste anything the insect lands on.

CATERPILLARS

ZOOM BUBBLE

What is a caterpillar? It's a young butterfly. It hatches from an egg. Then it munches on leaves and stems.

After one or two weeks, this larva looks for a safe place. It sheds its skin and becomes a pupa.

LIFE CYCLE

A butterfly begins life inside an EGG.

A CATERPILLAR eats and grows, eats and grows.

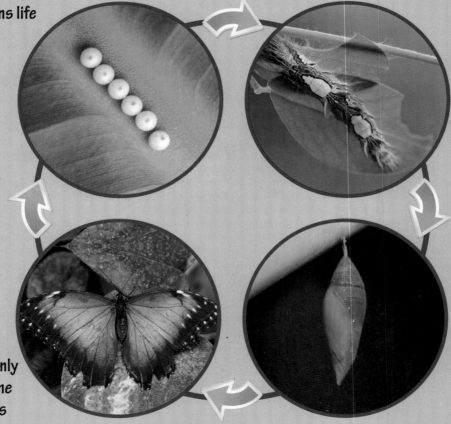

Most ADULT butterflies live only a few weeks. Some can live as long as ten months.

A butterfly PUPA rests in a chrysalis. While inside, its body is changing.

LEARN MORE

BOOKS

Bishop, Nic. *Butterflies and Moths*. New York: Scholastic, 2009.

Murawski, Darlyne. *Face to Face with Butterflies*. Washington, D.C.: National Geographic, 2010.

Rabe, Tish. *My, Oh My—A Butterfly!* New York: Random House Books for Young Readers, 2007.

WEB SITES

Butterflies and Moths of North America
<http://www.butterfliesandmoths.org/>

The Children's Butterfly Site
<http://www.kidsbutterfly.org/>

INDEX

Enslow Elementary, an imprint of Enslow Publishers, Inc.
Enslow Elementary® is a registered trademark of Enslow
Publishers, Inc.

Copyright © 2014 by Melissa Stewart

Library of Congress Cataloging-in-Publication Data
Stewart, Melissa.
    Zoom in on butterflies / Melissa Stewart.
        p. cm. — (Zoom in on insects!)
    Summary: "Provides information for readers about a
butterfly's home, food, and body"—Provided by publisher.
    ISBN 978-0-7660-4211-7
    1. Butterflies—Juvenile literature. I. Title. II. Series:
Stewart, Melissa. Zoom in on insects.
    QL544.2.S747 2014
    595.789—dc23
                                        2012040387

Future editions:
Paperback ISBN: 978-1-4644-0365-1
EPUB ISBN: 978-1-4645-1202-5
Single-User PDF ISBN: 978-1-4646-1202-2
Multi-User PDF ISBN: 978-0-7660-5834-7

Printed in the United States of America
102013 Lake Book Manufacturing, Inc. Melrose Park, IL
10 9 8 7 6 5 4 3 2 1

Series Literacy Consultant:
Allan A. De Fina, PhD
Past President of the New Jersey Reading Association
Dean, College of Education
New Jersey City University
Jersey City, New Jersey

Photo Credits: Artyom Rudenko/Photos.com, p. 10; David M.
Phillips Ph.D./Science Source, p. 13; Gary Boisvert/Photos.com,
p. 8; Hans Christoph Kappel/NPL/Minden Pictures, p. 14; Ingo
Arndt/NPL/Minden Pictures, p. 19; lrh847/Photos.com, p. 4;
pjgs/Photos.com, p. 12; Shutterstock.com, pp. 1, 2, 3, 5, 6, 7, 9,
11, 15, 16, 17, 20, 21, 22; Ziga Camernik/Photos.com, p. 18.

Cover Photo: Shutterstock.com

Enslow Elementary
an imprint of
Enslow Publishers, Inc.
40 Industrial Road
Box 398
Berkeley Heights, NJ 07922
USA
http://www.enslow.com

Science Consultant:
Helen Hess, PhD
Professor of Biology
College of the Atlantic
Bar Harbor, Maine